C INSTRUMENTS

THE BILLY COBHAM REAL BOOK

For more info on the Real Book series, including community forums,
please visit **www.officialrealbook.com**.

ISBN 978-1-4950-9972-4

7777 W. BLUEMOUND RD. P.O. BOX 13819 MILWAUKEE, WI 53213

Visit Hal Leonard Online at
www.halleonard.com

THE BILLY COBHAM REAL BOOK

AC/DC

By Billy Cobham

CROSSWIND

BY BILLY COBHAM

THE DANCER

By Billy Cobham

DESICCATED COCONUTS

By Billy Cobham

HEATHER

By Billy Cobham

LE LIS

By Billy Cobham

LIGHT AT THE END OF THE TUNNEL

By Billy Cobham

MIRAGE

By Billy Cobham

Moon Germs

By Billy Cobham

64

OBLIQUELY SPEAKING

By Billy Cobham

PANAMA

By Billy Cobham

Go back to one (1) bar before Letter "B" for beginning of next solo

THE PLEASANT PHEASANT

By Billy Cobham

SOLOS ARE BASED AROUND 8ᵇ MINOR HERE

DRUM SOLO STARTS AT LETTER "F" TO LETTER "G"

Radioactive

By Billy Cobham

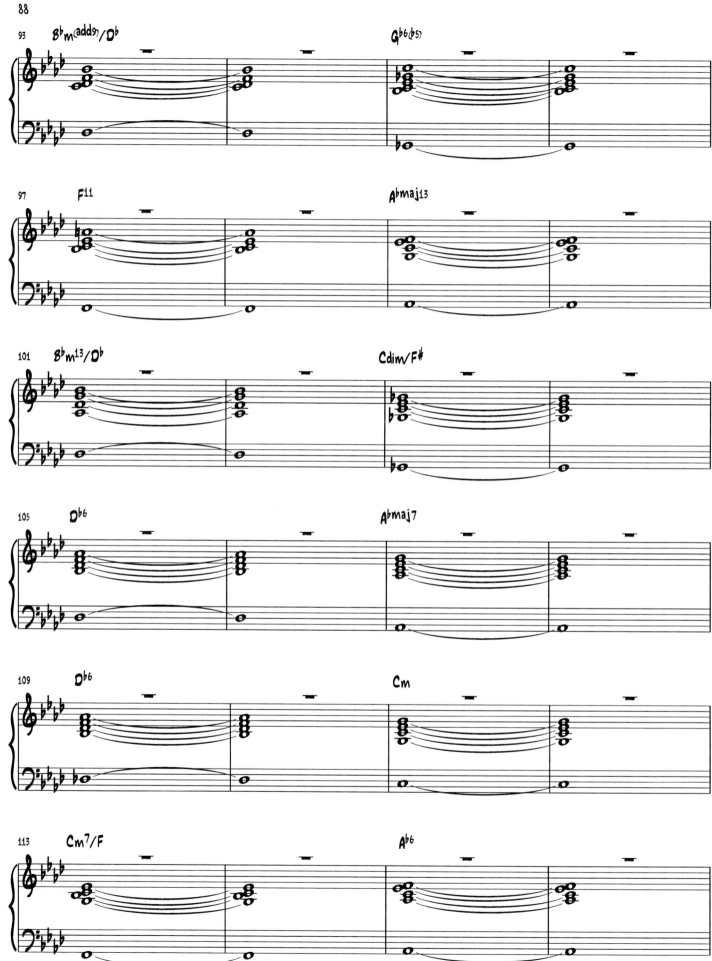

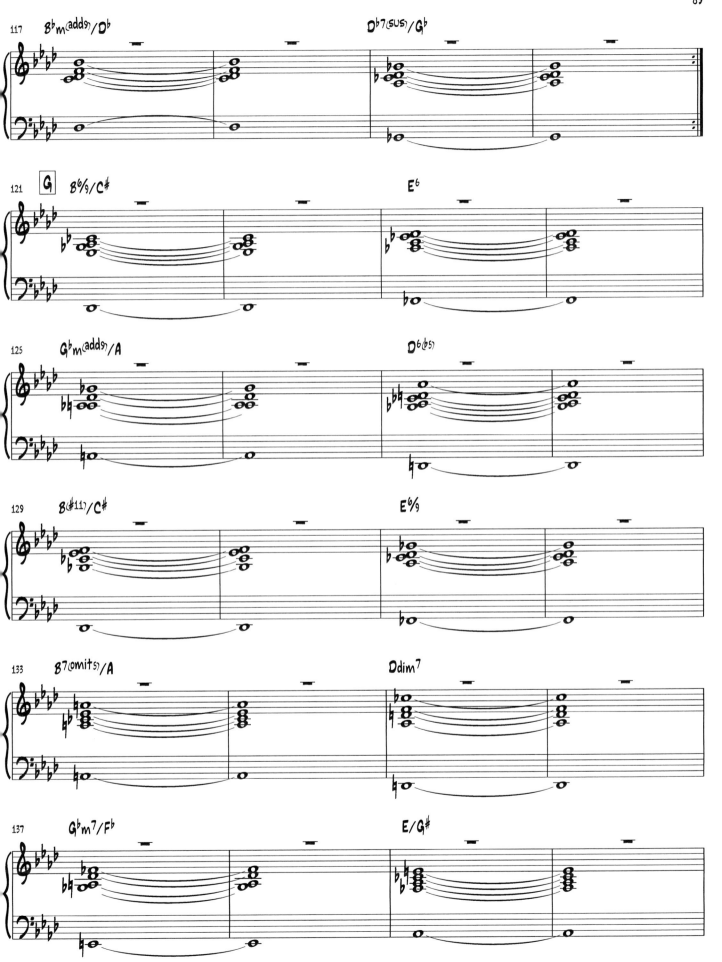

Red Baron

By Billy Cobham

STRATUS

By Billy Cobham

This is the vamp on the waay out of the tune!
Drum solo on the vamp out!

TO THE WOMAN IN MY LIFE

By Billy Cobham